Elliott Carter

Retracing III

for Trumpet in B-flat

Archive Edition

HENDON MUSIC

BOOSEY & HAWKES

AN IMAGEM COMPANY

DISTRIBUTED BY

HAL•LEONARD®
CORPORATION
7777 W. BLUEMOUND RD. P.O. BOX 13819 MILWAUKEE, WI 53213

www.boosey.com
www.halleonard.com

TRUMPET in B♭

RETRACING III

Elliott Carter

Printed 7 December 2009